ENIGMAS *of* HISTORY

THE MYSTERY OF MACHU PICCHU

WORLD
BOOK

a Scott Fetzer company
Chicago
www.worldbook.com

World Book edition of "Enigmas de la historia" by Editorial Sol 90.

Enigmas de la historia
La ciudad de Machu Picchu

This edition licensed from Editorial Sol 90 S.L.
Copyright 2013 Editorial Sol S.L. All rights reserved.

English-language revised edition copyright 2015
World Book, Inc.
Enigmas of History
The Mystery of Machu Picchu

World Book, Inc.
233 North Michigan Avenue, Suite 2000
Chicago, Illinois 60601 U.S.A.

For information about other World Book publications,
visit our website at **www.worldbook.com** or call
1-800-967-5325.

Library of Congress Cataloging-in-Publication Data

Ciudad de Machu Picchu. English.
The mystery of Machu Picchu.
     pages cm. -- (Enigmas of history)
 Originally published: La ciudad de Machu Picchu.
Editorial Sol 90 S.L., [2013].
   Includes Index.
   Summary: "An exploration of the questions scholars
have concerning Machu Picchu, an Inca archaeological
site in Peru. Features include, fact boxes, biographies of
famous experts on the Inca and Machu Picchu, places
to see and visit, a glossary, further readings, and index"
-- Provided by publisher.
   ISBN 978-0-7166-2675-6
   1. Machu Picchu Site (Peru)--Juvenile literature.
2. Incas--Juvenile literature. I. World Book, Inc. II.
Title.
F3429.1.M3C58 2015
985'.37--dc23
                              2015009348
Enigmas of History Set ISBN: 978-0-7166-2670-1

Printed in China by Shenzhen Donnelley
Printing Co., Ltd., Guangdong Province
1st printing May 2015

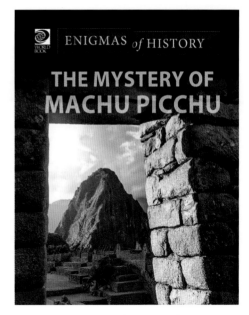

The peak Huayna Picchu looms over the ruins
of Machu Picchu.

© Kseniya Ragozina, iStockphoto

Staff

Contents

The Enduring Mystery of Machu Picchu

Within the majestic landscape of Peru, in the Andes Mountains and near the Amazon rain forest, sits Machu Picchu. The site is among the greatest artistic and architectural achievements of the ancient world and is a monument to the greatness of Inca civilization.

Machu Picchu has long been famous for its beautiful ruins. The site contains some of the finest stonework in the world, perched on a sharp-edged ridge amidst a spectacular mountain landscape. It was no surprise when the United Nations Educational, Scientific and Cultural Organization (UNESCO) named Machu Picchu a World Heritage Site in 1983.

Visitors to Machu Picchu have the rare pleasure of walking among buildings little changed from the time of the Inca who built the city. The site is a virtual time capsule for *archaeologists* (scientists who study past cultures). The location was uninhabited before the Inca built Machu Picchu, and nothing has been built there since the site was abandoned. Archaeologists know that Machu Picchu was built and occupied over a span of fewer than 80 years.

Hiram Bingham, the American historian and explorer who first brought Machu Picchu to the public's attention in 1911, was disappointed that he did not find any Inca treasure at the site. But the bones and *artifacts* (human-made objects) he collected have provided scientists with a wealth of information about Inca culture. Yet, a key mystery still endures—what was the purpose of Machu Picchu?

Without written records, archaeologists are left only with the physical remains to help understand the site. Many imaginative theories, often lacking in solid evidence, have been proposed to explain how and why Machu Picchu was built. Some of these theories were outlandish and involved the ruins having been built by aliens or people from the legendary lost civilization of Atlantis. Archaeologists know these origin stories are impossible. They are more interested in how Machu Picchu compares to known Inca settlements and what the site tells them about Inca culture.

For some scholars, this means viewing Machu Picchu as part of a larger system involving other Inca ruins and their natural settings. They also examine how the site fits with Inca religious beliefs and practices within the surrounding landscape that was sacred to the Inca. Scholars know all of these to be closely associated with some of the most important aspects of Inca life: the fertility of the land for crops, the weather, the power held by rulers and priests, and trade. The Inca believed all of these were influenced by the stars and planets. At Machu Picchu, there are several buildings that suggest the city could have been an important astronomical *observatory* (place to view and study stars and planets).

Excavations (digging) within the ruins have been limited since Hiram Bingham's initial investigations. Much of the work at Machu Picchu has been done to restore and preserve the ruins, which have been damaged by storms, earthquakes, and tourist traffic over the years. Today, Machu Picchu is a popular tourist destination, especially among people who believe, as the Inca did, that the site has a special significance and possesses mystical powers.

Machu Picchu is the best known of many Inca sites located in the district of Vilcabamba in the Andes Mountains of Peru. This region is known for being the last hideout of the Inca as they attempted to escape the conquering Spaniards in the 1500's. Other Inca ruins in this region include Choquequirao and Espíritu Pampa, which are being restored and made more accessible to visitors.

For visitors, each return to Machu Picchu seems to reveal something new—a previously unnoticed pattern of stones, a natural feature incorporated into the architecture, or some other new detail that reveals something about life among the Inca 500 years ago. Scientists are still studying the evidence, and their research will continue to provide new information that will increase our understanding of the site. However, as scholars find answers to some questions surrounding Machu Picchu, new questions arise. Many people hope Machu Picchu will always remain a place of mystery.

HIDDEN

The ruins of Machu Picchu are found 7,874 feet (2,400 meters) above sea level, among the high Andean peaks and in the shadow of Huayna Picchu, the high peak that towers over the site.

The Lost City of the Inca

In the short history of the Inca empire—from the mid-1400's to 1532—Machu Picchu was a sacred *citadel* (high-walled fortress). It served as a royal retreat from the capital at Cusco, some 50 miles (80 kilometers) to the northwest. American historian Hiram Bingham rediscovered these centuries-old ruins for the world in 1911.

Between Lake Titicaca (TEE tee KAH kah) on the border of what are now Peru and Bolivia, and the Cusco valley at the foot of the Andes, a culture was born that rapidly grew to become one of the largest and richest empires in the Americas. At the height of its power, the Inca empire reached from what is now Ecuador, through Peru and Bolivia, to Chile and the northern part of Argentina. It was an immense territory that spanned almost 2,500 miles (4,023 kilometers) in length and 250 miles (403 kilometers) in width. Experts disagree about the population, but between 10 million and 30 million people may have made up the Inca empire. Since about A.D. 1200, these people were ruled by a *dynasty* (ruling family) from the capital in Cusco, which means "navel of the earth" in Quechua, the Inca language. Much of what we know about Inca culture comes from Spanish historian Garcilaso de la Vega (1539-1616) in his work *Primera Parte de los Comentarios Reales de los Incas* (The Royal Commentaries of Peru) published in 1609. However, there is no mention of Machu Picchu in this work.

There is a legend that on the Island of the Sun at Lake Titicaca, Manco Cápac and Mama Ocllo appeared. These two, the legendary founders of the Inca dynasty, were both brother and sister and husband and wife. The legend goes on to say that Manco Cápac planted his gold staff in the ground by the Tullumayo and Huatanay rivers. Here, he founded the city of Cusco from which the Inca empire rose. Between A.D. 1200 and 1438, Cusco was ruled by eight kings, called Inca: Manco Cápac, Sinchi Roca, Lloque Yupanqui, Mayta Cápac, Cápac Yupanqui, Inca Roca, Yahuar Huacac, and Hatun Topa, who was sometimes called Viracocha.

The nearby kingdom of Chanka threatened the power of the Cusco dynasty during Hatun Topa's reign. His son, Inca Yupanqui (reigned 1438-1471), conquered the Chanka and saved Cusco after his father fled. This son took the name *Pachacuti,* which means *earth shaker,* and built a large army. He is the 9th Inca and is recognized as the first Inca emperor. During his reign Machu Picchu was constructed in secret, perhaps to preserve its valuable political or religious nature. The Inca called their empire *Tawantinsuyu.*

In 1471, after years of expanding the Inca empire as a conqueror and statesman, Pachacuti gave up the role of emperor to his son Topa Inca Yupanqui, who conquered still more of the surrounding kingdoms. His son, Huayna Cápac, continued to expand the empire, even as he was forced to put down several uprisings that broke out against Inca rule. In 1525, he died of smallpox brought to the Americas by the first Spanish *conquistadors* (conquerors). His death served as advance notice of the Spanish army that would very soon arrive in Inca lands.

CIVIL WAR

Upon Huayna Cápac's death, a struggle for power broke out among his two sons, Huáscar and Atahualpa. Huáscar had the support of the Cusco nobility, but Atahualpa led the powerful northern army. In 1532, Atahualpa's troops occupied the city of Cusco and Huáscar was taken prisoner. The victor showed no mercy. Atahualpa ordered that his brother's entire family, which included many of his own relatives, be killed. He also ordered the execution of chiefs who supported Huáscar, even those who had been close friends.

In the middle of this civil war, in April 1531, Spanish conquistador Francisco Pizarro landed at the border between what are now Ecuador and Peru, leading a group of 200 men with some 70 horses. On November 15, 1532, Atahualpa and Pizarro arranged to meet at Cajamarca.

At the beginning of the meeting, Dominican friar Vicente Valverde, with a cross and a book in his hands, addressed Atahualpa and read the *Requerimiento*. This was an *ultimatum* (the final terms presented by one party) in which the Inca people would be required to recognize Spanish laws and accept Christianity. Atahualpa smacked the book out of the friar's hand in anger at such demands.

Valverde shouted that "the Indian chief has thrown the book of our holy laws to the ground!" as Pizarro's cavalry charged and soldiers opened fire. Thousands in the Inca army were killed in the resulting battle.

Pizarro took Atahualpa captive. He demanded that the Inca people fill three rooms with gold and silver in exchange for the emperor's freedom. It took months for the Inca people to collect the ransom. During this time, Atahualpa ordered the execution of his brother Huáscar. However, even as the Inca paid the ransom, Francisco Pizarro executed Atahualpa on August 29, 1533, leaving the Inca without an emperor.

In November 1533, Spanish soldiers took Cusco without opposition. The extraordinary network of Inca roads aided the success of the Spanish soldiers. American *archaeologist* (scientist who studies past cultures) John Hyslop calculated that approximately 14,409 miles (23,190 kilometers) of roads were built in the Inca empire. However, the Spanish did not find Machu Picchu, hidden in the sanctuary of the high Andes, and steal the treasures kept there. But the powerful Inca empire was centered in Cusco, and the capture of this city led to the empire's quick decline.

INCA SOCIETY

The Inca empire was composed of social classes that included commoners; a servant class; local nobles; and the royal court of Cusco. Within social classes, people were organized in groups called *ayllu*, based on both

PLATFORMS
The classic terraces of Inca agriculture are found in Machu Picchu (above, left).

ROYAL TOMB
Bingham named the natural cave (above, right) found below the Temple of the Sun the Royal Tomb, even though no mummy was found inside. The "tomb" has a staircase dug from the rock and stones molded in a fascinating way.

kinship and common land ownership. Priests were important in Inca society. The most powerful priests were often close relatives of the royal family. Priests made offerings, performed sacrifices, and maintained the temples. Religious ceremonies marked important calendar events as well as events in the life of a ruler. The Inca economy did not operate with money. Instead, the Inca state produced fine pottery, cloth, items of precious stones, and metalwork in silver, gold, and bronze that were used as gifts to keep the loyalty of local lords. The state also stockpiled food, weapons, and other goods to support the army and other workers. Inca subjects performed a labor tax, called *mita*, to make the food and supplies the Inca needed. The Inca's subjects also exchanged crafts, food, and other goods among themselves.

AN ABSOLUTE RULER

The ruling Inca was seen as the physical presence of the empire they called *Tawantinsuyu*, the Kingdom of the Sun. The Inca people believed that the world was created by the god Viracocha. The ruling family claimed descent from the sun, called Inti. The earth goddess, Pachamama, was one of the most important female gods, and the sea and the moon were also worshiped as goddesses.

The Inca regarded many places and objects as *huaca* (sacred). Mummies of important ancestors, temples, and historical places were all worshiped as huaca. Natural features on the landscape, such as springs, boulders, caves, and mountain peaks, were also sacred and called *apu*. Each household had one or more small statues, or *illa*, that were sacred as well.

Spanish conquerors tried to destroy the Inca customs and religion. Spanish officials served as "inspectors," responsible for visiting Inca communities to urge them to abandon the *idols* (image or other object that is worshiped as a god) of their native religion and convert to Christianity. The Spanish priest Pablo Joseph de Arriaga (1564-1622), who wrote *La extirpación de la idolatría en el Perú* (The removal of idolatry in Peru), shared a typical day's work. He wrote, "all of the *mallquis* (mummies of ancestors), and we found many of these, we burned. Among them two pairs of small silver cups were found, with which it appeared the Indians used to drink to the dead. At nightfall, we gave thanks to the Lord for our successes, having taken all of the idols and everything else we found."

Other idol inspectors acted with less consideration in the search for huacas and mallquis. The fury of these Spanish soldiers and priests would soon devastate what remained of the Inca empire.

THE INCA RESISTANCE

In Cusco, the Spaniards appointed Manco Inca—another son of Huayna Cápac—as the new ruler. But it was Pizarro who really was in control. Meanwhile, the Spaniards had to fight in several areas to put down resistance to their rule. Manco Inca eventually fled Cusco and organized a resistance. The rebel Inca forces took refuge in the city of Vilcabamba. Manco Inca besieged Cusco for 12 months, but he could not take the city back from the Spanish. The Inca continued to resist for more than 30 years, led by Manco Inca's sons Tito Cusi and later Túpac Amaru, the

last Inca emperor. In 1572, Francisco of Toledo, the Spanish viceroy of Peru, ordered a final assault on the Inca stronghold of Vilcabamba. He captured the city and executed Túpac Amaru in the Cusco Plaza. Thus, the Inca empire came to its end.

LOST CITIES OF THE INCA

Vilcabamba was enshrined in Inca *myth* (stories) as the last stronghold of the empire. Many tales about the Inca city grew and captured the imagination of American and European adventurers, explorers, and writers in search of fabled lost cities said to contain magnificent riches. In 1710, Spanish explorer Juan Arias Díaz Cañete stated "the news is true that by old traditions the riches of these areas can be had."

One of those inspired by the idea was American Hiram Bingham (1875-1956), an associate professor of South American history at Yale University. In 1906, he walked from Venezuela to Colombia, following the same Andean route taken by the great South American liberator Simón Bolívar in 1819. Two years later, Bingham followed the old trading route used by the Spaniards through the Andes from Buenos Aires in Argentina to Lima, Peru. His Peruvian adventure took him to the ruins of a place called Choquequirao, which, according to his native guides, had been the last capital of the Inca rebel forces. Bingham could see that Choquequirao was not the place he was looking for. In 1911, the historian returned to Cusco as director of an archaeological expedition for Yale University and entered the Urubamba Valley. On the morning of June 24, accompanied by a sergeant of the civil guard named Carrasco, Bingham climbed the cultivated *terraces* (platforms) of a farm owned by Melquíades Richarte and Anacleto

Antonio Raimondi
(1826-1890)

Born in Milan, this Italian naturalist arrived in Peru in 1850 and dedicated himself to the scientific study of the entire country. He traveled for almost 20 years all over Peru. Even though he died before the discovery of Machu Picchu, his studies helped to establish a foundation for understanding the Inca and other *pre-Columbian* (before the 1400's and the arrival of Columbus in the New World) cultures in Peru.

FORERUNNER Raimondi's influence on scientific knowledge of Peru is without measure. His greatest work is *El Perú*, in six volumes.

María Rostworowski
(1915-)

Daughter of a Polish father and a Peruvian mother, she is a leading expert on the Inca and other ancient Peruvian cultures. She studied with Peruvian historian Raúl Porras Barrenechea at the University of San Marcos. Her first published work was a study of Inca Pachacuti, who ordered the construction of Machu Picchu.

EXPERT Rostworowski's work has provided a richer and more complete view of Inca history.

Hiram Bingham (1875-1956)

Bingham was born to a family of Protestant missionaries in Honolulu, Hawaii, in 1875. He earned degrees from Yale, the University of California, and Harvard, although he never formally studied *archaeology* (scientific study of the remains of past human cultures). Bingham is credited with discovering Machu Picchu in 1911. In reality, local people and others knew of the site's existence. Bingham described three other important Inca archaeological sites— Choquequirao, Vitcos, and Vilcabamba. He believed that Machu Picchu was the last capital of the Inca, and that Vilcabamba was a lesser site. Actually, Vilcabamba was the capital. In 1948, he published *Lost City of the Incas,* a best-selling book about his expedition to Machu Picchu. He later served as a U.S. senator. Bingham is thought to have been an inspiration for the archaeologist "Indiana Jones," a character in a popular series of Hollywood movies.

DISCOVERER Bingham was not the first person to walk around Machu Picchu since the fall of the Inca empire. His great success was making the existence of this mysterious place known to the world and motivating archaeological investigation of the site.

> *"Without the slightest expectation of finding anything more interesting than the stone-faced terraces, I finally left the cool shade of the pleasant little hut and climbed farther up the ridge."*
>
> Hiram Bingham in *The Lost City of the Incas* (1948)

Johan Reinhard (1943-)

A specialist in pre-Columbian archaeology, as well as an expert mountain climber, Reinhard is responsible for some of the most significant discoveries of Andean mummies, including the mummy known as Juanita (found at the Ampato volcano, Peru, in 1995) and mummies known as the three Niños (children) del Llullaillaco (found at Salta, Argentina, in 1999). Reinhard published *Machu Picchu: The Sacred Center* (1999), which presented innovative theories about this archaeological site.

INNOVATOR Aside from his field discoveries, Johan Reinhard has suggested theories concerning the location of important Inca sites.

Before Bingham

Scholars do not know if any Spanish *conquistadors* (conquerors) ever arrived at Machu Picchu. If they did, it seems they made no mention of the *citadel* (walled fortress) in any records or accounts of their expeditions. However, scholars do know that several people visited Machu Picchu before 1911, when Hiram Bingham "discovered" the site. Almost a decade before Bingham's arrival, Cusco resident Agustín Lizárraga came across the site. Lizárraga marked one of the walls at Machu Picchu with his name and the date when he stumbled upon the site in 1901. Bingham saw this *graffiti* (words, drawings, or other marks scratched or painted on walls or other surfaces) and made a mention of it in the diary of his 1911 expedition.

In 2008, American cartographer Paolo Greer described evidence that Machu Picchu had been discovered and pillaged by a German adventurer named Augusto Berns, in 1867, more than 40 years before Bingham arrived. The evidence consists of a series of maps and registries that were found in Peru. Greer believes that Berns methodically extracted many treasures from the Inca ruins. This may explain why Bingham found so little gold and treasure among the well-built palaces and temples at Machu Picchu.

Regardless of the uncertainty about the first foreigner to set eyes upon Machu Picchu, scholars know that the site was not really "discovered" by anyone. Local farmers, descendants of the Inca, knew of the site and even used the terraced lanscape at Machu Picchi to grow their crops.

LATE ARRIVAL
Hiram Bingham's men explore Machu Picchu. Bingham made the ruins known worldwide, but others were there ahead of him.

Machu Picchu: not that unknown

In his work *Historia General del Qosqo* (1992), Peruvian historian José Tamayo Herrera cites a published record dated August 8, 1776, to show that Machu Picchu was not an unknown site. According to this document, two brothers named Ochoa paid 350 pesos to Mrs. Manuela Almirón Villegas for the "sites of Pijchu, Machupijchu and Huaynapijchu." The Ochoas later sold the land to the Chief Magistrate of the Urubamba Valley, Marco Antonio de la Cámara, in 1782. Thus, Herrera believes that Machu Picchu was a well-known location and even owned by some people over the years.

MISSING TREASURE
It is likely that any valuable treasures that were to be found at Machu Picchu were taken away before Hiram Bingham's arrival at the site in 1911. Such treasures may have included small statues, or *illa*, which were sacred. For the upper-class visitors to Machu Picchu, these statues were sometimes crafted of gold or silver.

Álvarez. Richarte's son, Pablito, then led Bingham to ruins covered in plants. The ruins were called "machu pikchu" in *Quechua*, the language of the Inca that is still spoken in the region today. Bingham recorded the name of the site as Machu Picchu.

With support from Yale University and the National Geographic Society, Bingham returned to Machu Picchu in 1912 and again in 1915 with a team of experts to conduct *excavations* (digging). Bingham mistakenly decided that Machu Picchu had been the last refuge of the Inca resistance instead of Vilcabamba, which he considered to be a site of only minor importance. Today, scholars know that the opposite is correct.

From years of study, scholars now understand that cool and comfortable Machu Picchu was probably used as a retreat for members of the Inca royal family when they were away from Cusco. It had palaces where royalty could stay and entertain. It also had houses for the farmers, weavers, guards, and servants who lived at the site and worked for the royal family. The buildings were made of granite and had steep thatch roofs to protect against frequent rains.

Machu Picchu also had important religious and *astronomical* (concerning the stars and planets) functions.

The Temple of the Sun in Machu Picchu has a stone called the *Intiwatana* that is mounted on a platform. The four faces of this stone are aligned with the four cardinal directions: north, south, east, and west. The stone functions as a calendar, because it casts shadows in precise locations. Shadows are cast at the *solstices* (one of the two moments each year when the sun is at either its northernmost or southernmost position), which mark the beginning of summer and winter. They are cast again at the *equinoxes* (either of the two moments each year when the sun is directly above Earth's equator), which mark the beginning of spring and autumn.

of roads leading to the hidden Inca city. The Inca Trail, from about 50 miles (80 kilometers) outside of Cusco to Machu Picchu, is the best known. In 1998, a side path was discovered that connects the citadel to the Urubamba River.

1 MODERN ROAD

The winding Hiram Bingham Highway unites the village of Aguas Calientes with the site of Machu Picchu. Today, a bus ascends the rocky, steep, zigzag trail to take tourists to Machu Picchu. Bingham attended the opening of the road bearing his name in 1948.

2 THE INCA ROUTE

This road, which the Inca used, streches from outside Cusco to Machu Picchu. On this road, one can see the *Intipunku*, or Door of the Sun, the ancient Inca checkpoint. From here, one gets the first view of Machu Picchu.

Centennial paths

The vast network of Inca roads extends for thousands of miles from Cusco, the capital, to the four parts of the Inca empire. Since the vast majority of the paths existed before the Inca, they often only had to improve what was there already. Chasquis, or Inca couriers, would run at high speeds on this network of roads to deliver messages.

③

 HUAYNA PICCHU
Facing Machu Picchu, the mountain peak Huayna Picchu, with its own temples and side paths, seems to be guarding the ancient citadel. Far below in the valley, the Urubamba River hugs the site on three sides.

The Urban Design

Machu Picchu was divided into two main zones: agricultural and *urban* (city). *Terraced* (land that rises up in steps) fields for growing crops covered much of the agricultural section. The large main plaza was the center of the urban zone. As seen in other Inca cities, Machu Picchu's urban section had a *hanan* (sacred district) and a *hurin* (residential district).

Imperial Residence

Most researchers agree that it was Pachacuti, founder of *Tawantinsuyu* (the Inca empire), who ordered the construction of Machu Picchu as a royal retreat for refuge during winter.

Location
About 74 miles (119 kilometers) from Cusco, the capital of the Inca Empire, and 745 miles (1,200 kilometers) from Lima, the modern capital of Peru

Distribution
A step, a wall, and a *moat* (a deep, wide ditch dug around a castle or town as a protection against enemies), which also served as a drainage channel, separate the agricultural area from the urban area.

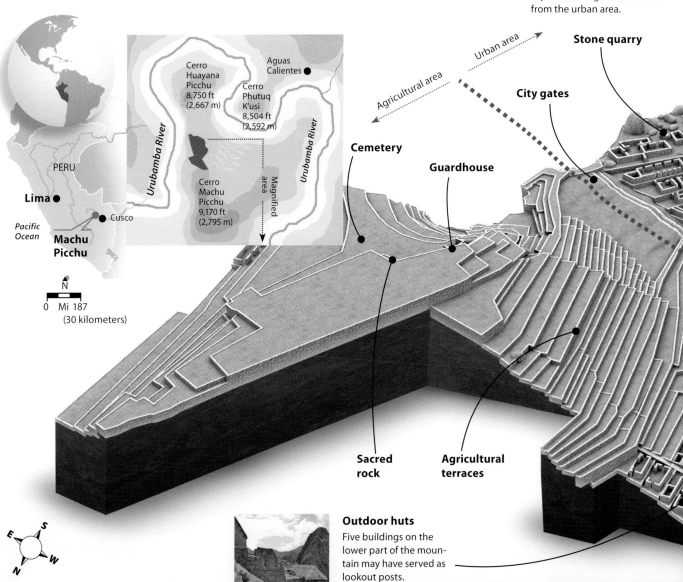

PERU

Lima ●

● Cusco

Pacific Ocean

Machu Picchu

N

0   Mi 187
     (30 kilometers)

Cerro Huayana Picchu
8,750 ft
(2,667 m)

Cerro Phutuq K'usi
8,504 ft
(2,592 m)

Aguas Calientes ●

Urubamba River

Urubamba River

Magnified area

Cerro Machu Picchu
9,170 ft
(2,795 m)

Urban area

Agricultural area

Stone quarry

City gates

Cemetery

Guardhouse

Sacred rock

Agricultural terraces

S
E   N
   W

Outdoor huts
Five buildings on the lower part of the mountain may have served as lookout posts.

What Purpose Did the Funerary Rock Have for Machu Picchu?

Large stones had great religious significance for the Inca. At Machu Picchu, there are special stones at the Temple of the Condor and the Temple of the Sun, among other spots. Funerary (burial) Rock, also known as the Ceremonial Rock, has a polished surface with steps and a ring carved into the rock. Some scholars believe this rock was used for preparing royal mummies.

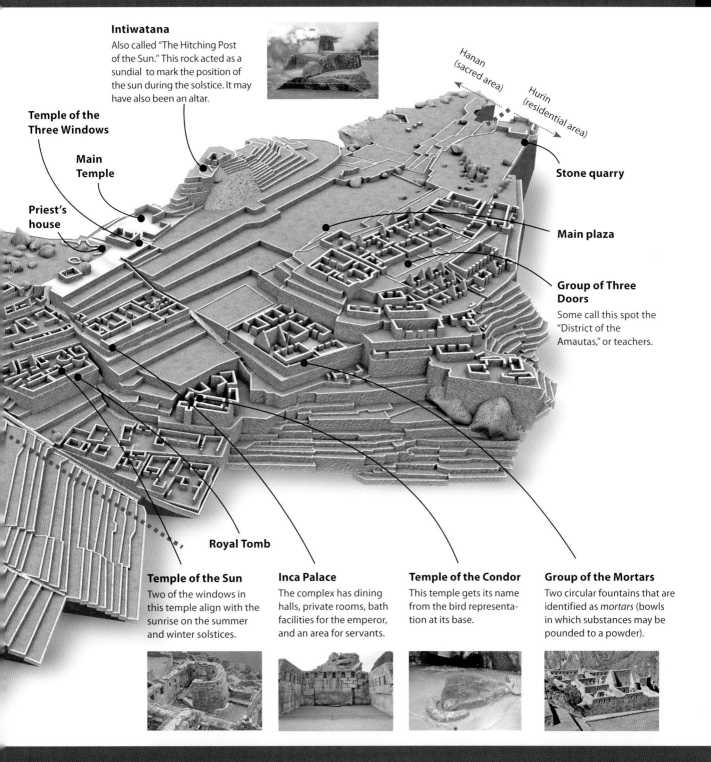

Intiwatana
Also called "The Hitching Post of the Sun." This rock acted as a sundial to mark the position of the sun during the solstice. It may have also been an altar.

Hanan (sacred area)

Hurin (residential area)

Temple of the Three Windows

Main Temple

Priest's house

Stone quarry

Main plaza

Group of Three Doors
Some call this spot the "District of the Amautas," or teachers.

Royal Tomb

Temple of the Sun
Two of the windows in this temple align with the sunrise on the summer and winter solstices.

Inca Palace
The complex has dining halls, private rooms, bath facilities for the emperor, and an area for servants.

Temple of the Condor
This temple gets its name from the bird representation at its base.

Group of the Mortars
Two circular fountains that are identified as *mortars* (bowls in which substances may be pounded to a powder).

How Was Machu Picchu Built?

Machu Picchu was constructed under the direction of Inca Pachacuti, founder of *Tawantinsuyu*, the Inca empire. It is a masterpiece of Inca architecture, a magnificent stone monument surrounded by a majestic natural landscape.

The *citadel* (walled fortress) of Machu Picchu was built on the slopes of the Vilcabamba mountain range, flanked by the Urubamba River. The Inca architects were well prepared to build upon the rugged land of the area, which featured nearly vertical slopes and deep gorges. These architects had gained experience from many Inca settlements in the Andes Mountains. The Inca carved out *terraces*, or flat steps of land, from the steep mountainsides. The flat surfaces could then be built upon or used for growing crops, including corn and potatoes. The terraces helped to prevent rain from washing away soil and seeds. In Machu Picchu, the trees were cut down and a set of platforms built with *irrigation* (channels for watering plants) to supply water for the corn, fruits, and plants grown for medicines.

EXCELLENT STONEWORK

Inca builders were experts in the construction of sturdy temples and palaces made of stone. Enormous blocks of hard granite rock were cut so carefully that they fit together without cement to hold them together. Spanish conquerors were amazed by the manner in which Inca builders were able to shape hard granite stones, sometimes very large in size, into perfectly fitting walls for buildings.

The Inca did not have a system of money. Instead, people paid taxes to the state in the form of crops, textiles that they produced, and in the form of labor, called *mita*. According to tradition, as many as 20,000 mita laborers worked to build a fortress outside of Cusco. Building Machu Picchu must have required a similar work force of thousands of stonecutters who pounded stones into shape. Stone hammers were the main tools for this work. (Although the Inca worked soft metals, including silver and gold, they did not produce tools with such harder metals as iron.) The huge granite blocks were dragged from the quarries to the construction site miles away. The stone blocks were dragged with ropes on wooden rollers. The Inca did not use any carts or wheeled vehicles, which would have been of little use in the mountainous terrain. Some stones still have indents that were made to help workers grip them. Smaller stones were transported on the backs of llamas. Skilled craftsmen used *plumb lines* (a string or line with a weight attached to one end) and other instruments for leveling stones and measuring angles and distances for building walls. Once the rocks arrived at the work site, workers smoothed the stones with sand. They smoothed one block so that it's surface would be perfectly fitted with the stone next to it.

Shaping the Stones

The steps taken to give the building stones their precise shape were simple, but it took a lot of work.

1 EXTRACTION

Wooden wedges were driven into existing cracks in a stone to widen the crack.

2 SOFTENING

Water was poured onto the wooden wedge to expand it and deepen the crack until the rock split.

3 POLISHING

The stone was pounded to smooth its surface, and then it was polished with sand and water to give it a smooth finish.

Terraces and Construction

The urban sector of Machu Picchu was for the nobility and has temples and various administrative areas. The agricultural district on the other hand was wholly dedicated to growing crops. Even with the high number of terraces present at the site, all signs indicate that Machu Picchu did not grow enough crops to be self-sufficient.

Terraces

The agricultural area was made up of large *terraces* or flat platforms for growing crops on the side of the mountain.

- Upper terraces
- Lower terraces
- Urban area

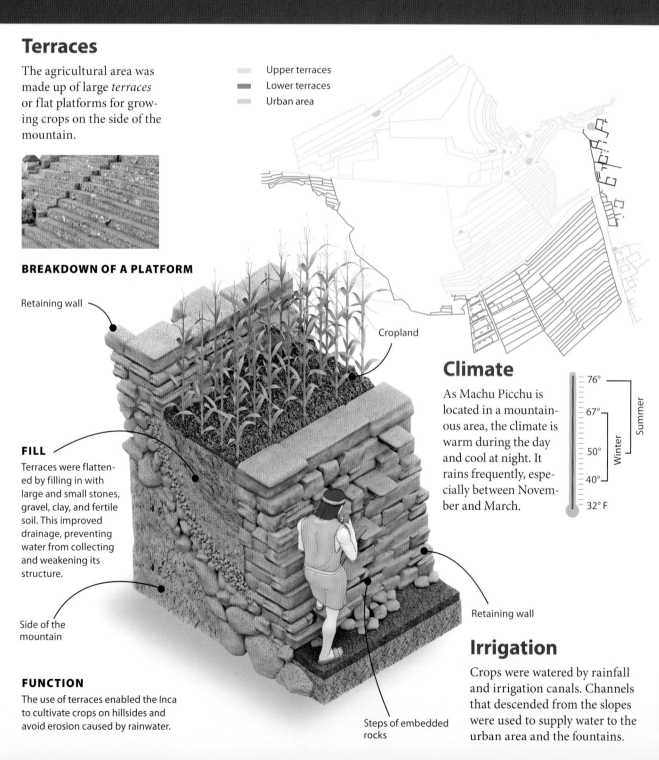

BREAKDOWN OF A PLATFORM

Retaining wall

Cropland

FILL
Terraces were flattened by filling in with large and small stones, gravel, clay, and fertile soil. This improved drainage, preventing water from collecting and weakening its structure.

Side of the mountain

FUNCTION
The use of terraces enabled the Inca to cultivate crops on hillsides and avoid erosion caused by rainwater.

Steps of embedded rocks

Retaining wall

Climate

As Machu Picchu is located in a mountainous area, the climate is warm during the day and cool at night. It rains frequently, especially between November and March.

76°
67°
50°
40°
32° F

Winter
Summer

Irrigation

Crops were watered by rainfall and irrigation canals. Channels that descended from the slopes were used to supply water to the urban area and the fountains.

What Was the Importance of the Location of the Farming Terraces?

Even though the agricultural sector covers half the surface area of Machu Picchu, experts think the cropland could only have produced enough to feed about 55 people, while the permanent population was at least 300. A recent examination of the terraces shows that they grew high value crops, like special varieties of corn and medicinal plants. These special crops would have been grown for the upper class members of society at Machu Picchu.

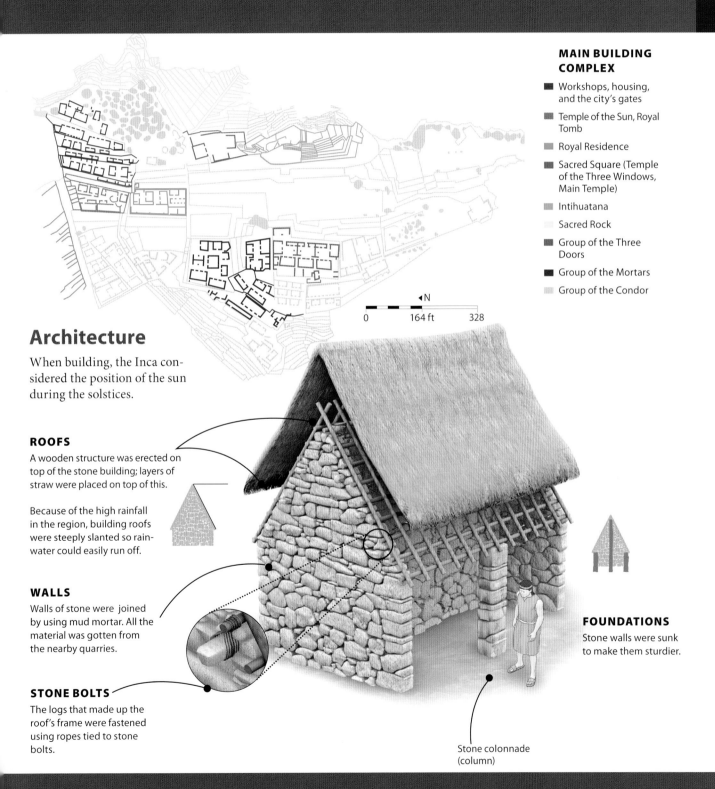

MAIN BUILDING COMPLEX

- Workshops, housing, and the city's gates
- Temple of the Sun, Royal Tomb
- Royal Residence
- Sacred Square (Temple of the Three Windows, Main Temple)
- Intihuatana
- Sacred Rock
- Group of the Three Doors
- Group of the Mortars
- Group of the Condor

◄ N

0   164 ft   328

Architecture

When building, the Inca considered the position of the sun during the solstices.

ROOFS

A wooden structure was erected on top of the stone building; layers of straw were placed on top of this.

Because of the high rainfall in the region, building roofs were steeply slanted so rainwater could easily run off.

WALLS

Walls of stone were joined by using mud mortar. All the material was gotten from the nearby quarries.

STONE BOLTS

The logs that made up the roof's frame were fastened using ropes tied to stone bolts.

FOUNDATIONS

Stone walls were sunk to make them sturdier.

Stone colonnade (column)

Was Machu Picchu a Sanctuary?

There are *documents* (papers) that show the close relationship that Pachacuti felt with the lands upon which Machu Picchu was built. It was his place of comfort and rest during his reign, and later a sacred location where his mummy would be worshipped.

The Inca regarded certain places and features of the landscape, such as springs, boulders, caves, and mountain peaks, as *apu*, or sacred. Mummies of ancestors, temples, and historical places were also all worshiped as *huaca*. Scholars believe that Machu Picchu, nestled in the shadow of two mountain peaks, Salcantay and the nearby Huayna Picchu, served as a unique site for the Inca worship of the dead, and especially of the founder of the Inca empire, Pachacuti.

In 1551, Spanish chronicler Juan de Betanzos provided a firsthand account of the relationship between Pachacuti, the first Inca emperor, and Machu Picchu in his *Suma y narración de los incas* (Narrative of the Inca). This written account is supported by the testimony of his wife Angelina Coya Yupanqui, a member of Inca nobility and one of Pachacuti's descendants. The chronicle confirms that Pachacuti's mummy was kept in a village he had had built for that purpose. However, *patallacta* is a Quechua word that simply means "village in the heights." Scholars think that Betanzos may have used this term to refer to Machu Picchu. They believe Pachacuti, the first Inca emperor, had Machu Picchu built as a holy *sanctuary* (sacred place), a site where his mummy could be worshipped after his death.

PLACE OF REST

Machu Picchu—Pachacuti's *patallacta*—seems to have also been his vacation home before it became his tomb. The city was constructed so the ruler could relax and yet still perform his official duties as emperor. From the streets of Machu Picchu, he could reach any of the four plazas or any of the temples and sacred locations in the citadel. Fountains, where the water flowed from the mountain summits and through stone *aqueducts* (water channels), decorated the open space between the central plaza and the main temple.

At Machu Picchu, Pachacuti would have been surrounded by people who helped to manage the empire. Inca royals were allowed to have more than one wife, and Pachacuti's main wife, or *coya*, would most likely accompany him to his retreat. Other members of the royal family, Pachacuti's advisors, priests, craftsmen, and servants, all needed to be housed at Machu Picchu.

Priests were housed around the main temple and the important Temple of Three Windows, made up of huge angular stones, finely sculpted and assembled to perfection. According to Bingham, the three windows of this temple relate to the Inca origin myth. The *amautas*, philosophers or wise men who advised the Inca ruler, were housed in another section. It is

In the Image of Nature

Some scholars have pointed out that Inca builders and sculptors seem to have been inspired by natural forms in the area. The sacred rock (below), known as Intiwatana, could be a copy of the form of the mountain Huayna Picchu, which is found behind it. Nearby is the compound of the Sacred Stone, marked by a single large block of stone which also appears to be a carbon copy of the mountains in front of it. From this stone, heading west by means of a steep path with steps carved in the rock and which crosses small agricultural terraces, the summit of Huayna Picchu can be reached. There in the heights of the "young mountain" a large stone can be seen in the shape of a throne, known as the "Inca chair." From this point, there is an incomparable view of the sanctuary, the Urubamba canyon, and the sacred mountains. On the north side, the mountain houses a cavern, similar to the royal tomb at the Temple of the Sun, connected to another farther up which has hollowed out places in the walls. This grouping of caves is known as the Temple of the Moon.

THE INTIWATANA
Its elevated location makes this stone an optimal place for astronomical observations.

Is Machu Picchu Lined Up with Other Cities?

In recent decades, scholars have recognized the symbolic importance of Inca sites in relation to the surrounding landscape and to other sites in the Inca empire. Mathematician and archaeologist María Scholten d'Ebneth discovered in 1977 that the Inca cities of Cajamarca, Machu Picchu, Ollantaytambo, Cusco, and Tiwanaku all appear aligned in a northwest-southeast direction. This forms a diagonal line of sacred value that is also seen in many crafts and objects in the cultures of the Andes. This line is called "Viracocha's Route," relating it to the mythical path taken by the Andean creator god from Tiwanaku to the Pacific Ocean.

recognized by high-walled buildings of reddish stone and decorated with cylinder-shaped stones protruding from the walls. Circular stone mortars used for making dyes, ceramics, and fabrics were found here, indicating that craftsmen also resided in this section. They made all of the items the emperor needed at this home away from the capital.

MOVING THE MUMMIES

The *mummies* (preserved bodies) of the Inca kings were maintained by their descendants in the palaces they lived in during life. After death, Pachacuti's mummy would have been kept at Machu Picchu. On occasion, royal mummies were brought to Cusco for important festivals. Historian Betanzos provides an

account of how the Inca worshipped the mummies of their past rulers.

Inca religious festivals were held at specific times of year based on the movements of the sun and moon. One important festival was the Capac Raymi. It took place at the summer *solstice*. In Peru, which lies south of the equator, the summer solstice occurs in December. The most important festival was the Inti Raymi, held around the winter solstice in June. On this day, the sun appears at its lowest point in the sky, and the period of daylight is shortest. The Inti Raymi was held to persuade the sun to not withdraw any farther from Earth. These ceremonies included several days of dancing, feasts, games, songs, and parades.

Betanzos describes an Inca festi-

val where the mummy of Pachacuti was carried in a long procession into the city of Cusco. The mummy was placed with other mummies of the kings that ruled before him in the Temple of the Sun at Cusco. Once the festival concluded, the mummies were returned to the places they were kept. Betanzos did not describe how Pachacuti's mummy was returned to the sanctuary of Machu Picchu, since the site was kept hidden from the Spanish by the secretive Inca priests.

The Inca continued to worship royal mummies after the Spanish conquest of Peru. Spanish authorities saw this worship as a threat to their political power and the Christian religion. They sought out and destroyed all the mummies of royals and high-ranking nobles that they

THREE WINDOWS

The Temple of the Three Windows (left) actually had five openings. Those on either end were filled in by the Inca themselves. The windows are the largest of any building ever constructed by the Inca. Between the windows, pottery fragments were found, which suggests the ceremonial breaking of vessels may have taken place here.

TEMPLE OF THE CONDOR

The Temple of the Condor (right) owes its name to a rock protruding from the ground at the site which has the appearance of a condor drinking from a circular fountain. The temple has many underground passages and water sources. Until recently some scholars believed that this building functioned as a prison, but today most understand it had a religious function.

could find. Today, scholars are not sure what became of Pachacuti's mummy. Some experts think that the Inca decided to move Pachacuti's mummy away from Machu Picchu—along with the mummies of his *coya* (main wife) and others—before the Spanish could discover the sanctuary.

However, another writer, Polo de Ondegardo, describes how the bodies of Pachacuti, the Inca king Huayna Cápac, and his wife, Mama Ocllo, were discovered in a house at Cusco. At the request of the local Spanish Viceroy, the bodies were given a Catholic burial at San Andrés, a hospital in the Peruvian capital of Lima. Today, no royal mummies of the Inca are known to exist. However, the Spanish never seemed to have discovered Pachacuti's sanctuary at Machu Picchu.

The Torreón, or Temple of the Sun

This temple is the only circular structure at Machu Picchu, and it functioned as a solar observatory. Its architecture represents some of the finest work in all Inca construction. Under the building, there is the Royal Tomb, where the mummy of the Inca Pachacuti is thought to have rested.

The Treasures of the Inca

Machu Picchu is a colossal testimony to the Inca's architectural abilities. Their ingenuity and skill, however, spill over into other forms of artistic expression: textiles, ceramics, goldsmithing, and ornaments made from other materials, which bear witness to their competence as artisans.

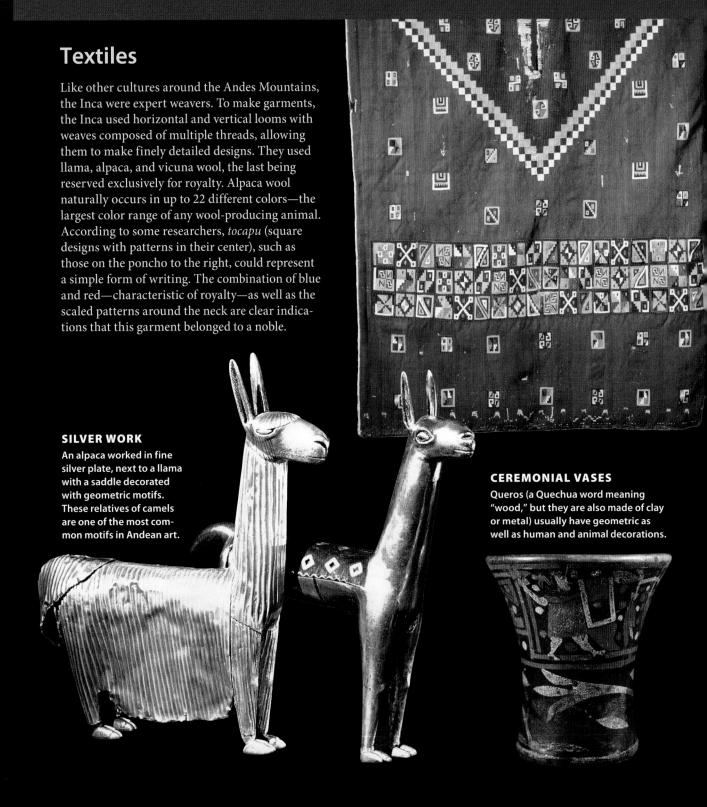

Textiles

Like other cultures around the Andes Mountains, the Inca were expert weavers. To make garments, the Inca used horizontal and vertical looms with weaves composed of multiple threads, allowing them to make finely detailed designs. They used llama, alpaca, and vicuna wool, the last being reserved exclusively for royalty. Alpaca wool naturally occurs in up to 22 different colors—the largest color range of any wool-producing animal. According to some researchers, *tocapu* (square designs with patterns in their center), such as those on the poncho to the right, could represent a simple form of writing. The combination of blue and red—characteristic of royalty—as well as the scaled patterns around the neck are clear indications that this garment belonged to a noble.

SILVER WORK

An alpaca worked in fine silver plate, next to a llama with a saddle decorated with geometric motifs. These relatives of camels are one of the most common motifs in Andean art.

CEREMONIAL VASES

Queros (a Quechua word meaning "wood," but they are also made of clay or metal) usually have geometric as well as human and animal decorations.

Sacrificial Knives

Ceremonial knives called *tumis* have a semicircular blade and a handle with a figure carved into it, usually the image of a god. These knives are found throughout the Andes and were made by many peoples prior to the Inca. They were used in religious sacrifices. They were usually made from a single sheet of metal.

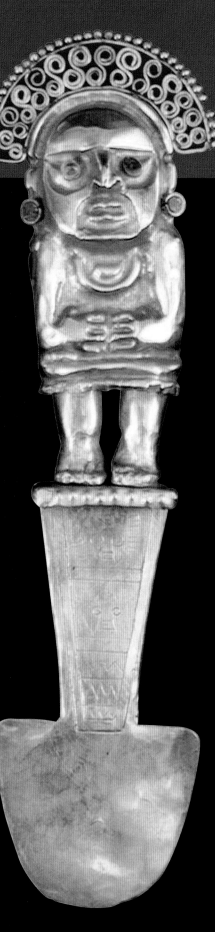

Sacred Plants

A highly realistic Incan representation of an ear of corn (above) crafted in silver. Corn was a rare luxury crop for the Inca, as the mountainous terrain of the Andes is not favorable for growing corn, and production was restricted to the valleys.

The Inca used corn to make chicha, an alcoholic drink used in rituals which is still very popular in the Andes today. Mills that were probably used to prepare chicha are found in Machu Picchu.

COLORED PLUMES
Magnificent fabrics, ornaments, and figurines were made by the Inca using the beautiful feathers from the Amazon region.

The Ceremony of the Sun

June 21—the shortest day of the year —was the most important day for the Inca. That day, they celebrated the Festival of the Sun, dedicated to the god Inti. The royal family and priests prepared for this ceremony, the largest and most important one of the year, with solemn prayer and fasting in the days leading up to the festival.

Natural cycles

Since they were a farming society, the Inca required exact knowledge of the cycles of nature. Thus, the winter *solstice*, which in the Southern Hemisphere is on June 21, was named the Festival of the Sun and became the most important Inca celebration. The festival lasted for several days and included parades, dances, songs, and animal sacrifices to ensure a good harvest. This illustration depicts how this festival might have looked in Machu Picchu.

The Winter Solstice

During the winter solstice at Machu Picchu, the rays of the sun would shine through the east window of the Temple of the Sun. The sun's rays would fall on the sacred rock which filled almost all of the enclosure. A precise groove cut into the rock was lit by the rays streaming in through the window on this day, proving that the Inca temple also served as a solar calendar.

KEY LOCATIONS FOR THE FESTIVAL OF THE SUN

1 ENTRANCE
Llamas, carrying food and various items for the festivities, entered through the main gate toward the storehouses.

2 INTIWATANA
This rock, "The hitching post of the sun," was fundamental in the celebration of the winter solstice. A stairway unites this location with the Main Square.

3 UNFINISHED TEMPLE
An area for worship in the initial stages of construction remained unfinished due to the sudden abandonment of the city.

4 MAIN SQUARE
The only open space of the complex. This is where the festivities took place, and it was also the meeting place in Machu Picchu.

5 TEMPLE OF THE SUN
Exclusively for use by royalty. The construction of this temple showed the precise arrival of the winter solstice.

Who Were the Virgins of the Sun?

A select group of women, often of royal blood and chosen for their beauty, took a vow to serve the sun god Inti. These women were the Virgins of the Sun, a term coined by the Spanish conquistadors.

The Virgins of the Sun is the term the Spanish used for the women known as *acllas* (chosen women) by the Inca. Pachacuti, the first Inca emperor, created this exclusive group dedicated to the cult of Inti, the sun god.

The acllas were selected by special officials, called *apu panaca*, who traveled throughout the Inca empire in search of girls 8 to 12 years old. The girls were selected for their great beauty and purity. Many were the daughters of local chieftains or the noble families of Cusco. The girls were then locked up in a building called *acllahuasi*, which means *residence of the chosen women*. The main acllahuasi at Cusco was built where the Christian Convent of Saint Catherine stands today. This building in Cusco served as a model for those built in other important cities throughout the Inca empire.

At the acllahuasi, the acllas spent years learning to weave, sew, cook, and to make *chicha*, an alcoholic drink made from corn fermented in sweetened water, and *zancu*, a type of bread made with corn and the blood of llamas. This food and drink served as a divine offering during the Inti Raymi festivals in June, the month when sacrifices were made to the sun. Acllas also made the clothes for mummies and priests.

AT THE SERVICE OF THE SUN

After four years of training, an aclla could become a priestess. As a priestess, she would play an important part in Incan ceremonies for the rest of her life. Inca priests and priestesses were vital to society. The emperor based his right to rule on a religious idea that the emperor was the representative of the sun god, Inti, and so ruled by divine right. Priestesses dedicated their entire lives to the service of the sun god and caring for the royal Inca mummies at temples.

Some historians from the period after the Spanish conquered the Inca used the term "Virgins of the Sun" for all women living in the acllahuasi. However, Peruvian *archaeologist* (scientist who studies past cultures) Federico Kauffmann Doig observed, "Only a small group of acllas were chosen to remain forever in the acllahuasi. They were called *mamacona*, and the role of these older acllas was to instruct the novice acllas, run the acllahuasi, and act as priestesses." Other aclla were allowed to give up their status as chosen women and marry. Thus, some historians use the term "Virgin of the Sun" exclusively for the mamaconas, the few who dedicated their entire lives to the service of the sun god, Inti, rather than all those who resided at the acllahuasi.

Mostly Feminine

Between 1912 and 1915, Hiram Bingham and his team discovered more than 100 tombs around Machu Picchu. Of these, 52 were excavated under the direction of George F. Eaton, an *osteologist* (scientist who studies human skeletons) from Yale University. Others were excavated by local residents who lived near Machu Picchu. After examining the human remains from these tombs, Bingham and Eaton realized that most of the skeletons found were of women. Bingham proposed the theory that this sacred place had been the final burial ground for the Virgins of the Sun who took refuge in the mountains of Vilcabamba before the fall of Cusco to the hands of the Spanish conquistadors. However, Peruvian archaeologist Luis G. Lumbreras referenced papers from the 1500's that tell of many acllahuasi established in the Urubamba Valley. He believes the bones belong to the many mamaconas and servants who would have lived at Machu Picchu during the time of the Inca.

VIRGINS OF THE SUN

Statuette of an Inca priestess, or mamacona (left).

An illustration of an Inca chosen woman, or aclla, in ceremonial dress (right).

What Was Life in the *Acllahuasi* Like?

The acllas were always locked up, and no one could see them except the Inca's *coya* (main wife) and her daughters, who checked to see whether or not everything was in order. As a result of this isolation, the acllas only interacted among themselves. There were men who were responsible for security and other special tasks, usually outside the sheltered area of the *acllahuasi*. These guards were known as *punku kamayu*. Any inappropriate behavior by these guards towards the Virgins of the Sun was invariably punished by death.

CEREMONIAL VASE

The food and drink destined for ceremonies to honor the god Inti were prepared in the acllahuasi. *Queros* were pitchers for drink offerings and other rituals.

Were Some Inca Mummies Child Sacrifices?

Human sacrifice may have been the most sacred Inca ritual. The most desired offerings were physically perfect children. Some were destined for the "high sanctuaries" on mountain peaks.

Spanish historical accounts from Peru during the 1500's describe certain Inca ceremonies that involved *mallqui*, a Quechua word meaning *seed* and *ancestor* that also refers to a *mummy*. The Inca preserved the bodies of their dead rulers and other important members of the nobility. These mummies were occasionally taken from their sanctuaries during festivals, and offerings of food and *chicha* (fermented corn drink) made to them.

The remains of commoners were also sometimes made into mummies. Commoners were often buried in mummy bundles. A bundle might contain one or several bodies. Each body was wrapped in cotton, and it dried naturally. These mummies were buried with clothing, food, weapons, and other valuables. The amount and quality of the goods placed in these burials depended on the rank of the individual at his or her time of death. Inca royals were not buried in such bundles.

OFFERINGS TO THE GODS

The Capac Hucha festival took place when a new Inca ruler came to the throne or when it was time to plant or harvest crops. The festival's name means "royal obligation." Children from throughout the empire were chosen by local officials for their beauty and sent to Cusco. On the appointed day, they were gathered together in Cusco's central plaza. Then the children were sent from Cusco to a sacred mountain site, where they were sacrificed and sent to the gods as messengers. The children were drugged before their death and most probably died of exposure to the cold.

Between 1995 and 1999, American *archaeologist* (scientist who studies past cultures) Johan Reinhard discovered the naturally mummified remains of 14 Inca human sacrifices at various sites on the peaks of several mountains in the Andes around Peru and Argentina. Reinhard found frozen mummies of both boys and girls, with offerings. Other burial sites, visited in the past by daring grave robbers, were empty. In one of the graves, a thick layer of volcanic ash was found. This led archaeologists to speculate that the Inca offered sacrifices on the mountain peaks in response to volcanic eruptions.

Probably the most famous Inca mummy is "Juanita," who is also known as the Ice Maiden. The frozen remains of this girl were found at Mount Ampato in 1995. When doctors performed a *computed tomography* (CT) scan on her body in 1996, they learned what had caused this girl's death. Usually such sacrifice victims were drugged and then died of exposure to the cold. This girl died of a head injury—she was killed with a club and then arranged in her grave. The scientists do not know why her death was different. Today, "Juanita" is kept at a museum in Peru, in a glass box that maintains a cold temperature to prevent the body from thawing.

Maybe They Weren't Human Sacrifices?

Some people have argued that the mummified children found at sites in the high Andes are not the victims of Inca sacrifice. Katia Gibaja, a descendant of the Inca and head of the Andean Information Branch of the Museum of High-Altitude Archaeology in Salta, Argentina, has argued that the concept of "sacrifice" does not exist in Quechua, the language of the Inca. She claims that with the arrival of the Spanish invaders, "burying their loved ones on the high mountains was how the Inca protected them from death. They believed that someday, in some way, they would awaken."

REST WITHOUT PEACE
The exhibition of Inca mummies has caused controversy among scientists, tourists, and the descendants of the Inca.

Capacocha

In the Inca ritual known as *capacocha*, children were sarificed to the Sun, the Moon, the royal dead, and the reigning Inca. The mummy of one victim, known as *La Doncella* (The Maiden), discovered near the peak of the Llullaillaco volcano, is now on display in a museum in Salta, Argentina. Scientists found that she was about 13 years old when Inca priests left her to freeze to death with two other children as a sacrifice to the gods more than 500 years ago. The scientists found evidence that the victims had been drugged before their death. The cold at the high elevation helped preserve her features in exquisite detail.

High-Altitude Archaeology

A Swiss expedition that ascended Mount Chañi in Argentina in 1901 was the first to climb a mountain in the Andes and find evidence of Inca rituals. Since then, high-altitude archaeology has allowed scientists to discover Inca mummies buried in high sanctuaries of the Andean mountains.

Cemeteries on High

Mountaintop burials are another of the surprising feats of the Inca. Some graves have been found at heights surpassing 20,000 feet (6,096 meters). The Inca reached these heights some 400 years before modern climbers for the purpose of performing the ritual human sacrifice, usually of children, on the chosen mountain peaks, a supremely sacred act. The children were carried in a solemn ceremony from Cusco to their final destination. American archaeologist and mountaineer Johan Reinhard led the teams that found the mummy Juanita in 1995 on Mount Ampato in Peru, and three mummified children in 1999 on the volcano Llullaillaco in Argentina.

Route to the Top

The Llullaillaco expedition took place in three stages: the climb to base camp, at 16,000 feet (4,877 meters); from base camp to Camp One, at 20,000 feet (6,096 meters); and from Camp One to the place of burial, at 22,000 feet (6,706 meters), nearly on the summit at 22,100 feet (6,736 meters).

LLULLAILLACO EXPEDITION

1 EXCAVATION
Once at the site, the Reinhard expedition began the excavation using archaeological tools and techniques. Accessing the remains was very difficult.

2 DISINTERMENT
Once the three mummies had been located, Reinhard and his team proceeded to carefully uncover them. They discovered that the state of preservation was almost perfect.

3 PROTECTION
To protect the hundreds-of-years-old bodies and keep them intact, the team wrapped the mummies in snow and foam rubber sheets.

4 DESCENT
During descent, the mummies were strapped to the archaeologist's backs. Trucks full of dry ice then transported the mummies to their final destination in the city of Salta.

The Mummies of Llullaillaco

The three mummies rest in special preservation chambers at a temperature of -2 °F (-19 °C)—similar to that of the mountain heights—in the Museum of High-Altitude Archaeology in Salta, Argentina.

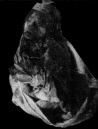

LIGHTNING GIRL
Named thus because her body was struck by lightning sometime after her death, she was only 6 years old.

THE MAIDEN
She is believed to have been about 13 years old. She wore a wool headdress with white feathers that is now exhibited separately.

THE BOY
He was found tied up with his head between his knees. He was about 7 years old, and there is evidence of blood on his clothes.

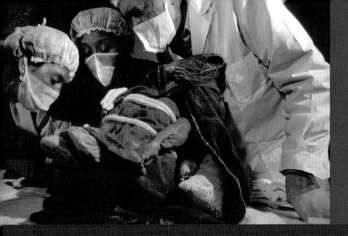

Temperature control

Scientists examine the mummy Juanita. The mummy is preserved in a glass capsule at the museum in Arequipa, Peru. The temperature of the capsule is maintained at a constant -2ºF (-19ºC).

HAIR

The hair was carefully combed, and two thin braids come down over the forehead. Some two dozen items were found near the body.

ORNAMENTS

A metal plate adorned Lightning Girl's head. The lightning strike left her face exposed on the mountain peak.

SMOOTH SKIN

Despite having been struck by lightning on her shoulder, chest, and ear, Lightning Girl's skin was extraordinarily well-preserved.

Quipus, Mysterious Inca Writing?

The Inca used knotted cords called *quipu* to keep track of crops, textiles, and other goods. However, some scholars think they are a form of writing used to record other information.

The Inca did not have an alphabetic writing system with which to keep records. According to the descriptions of Spanish conquerors, the Inca used quipus (*kee poos*) to record the goods and services they received as *tribute* (forced payment) from the peoples they ruled. *Quipu* means *knot* in Quechua, the language of the Inca and other people of the Andes Mountains. The Inca used quipus to keep records of crops, wool, textiles, building supplies, and other goods that were produced in the vast empire.

Scholars believe that the most widespread use of quipus occurred around the 1400's and early 1500's, during the height of the Inca empire. Quipus were made of knotted wool or cotton cords of one color or multiple colors. A typical quipu consists of a single main cord to which one or more pendant, or hanging cords are attached. A pendant cord may also have secondary cords attached to it. These cords, in turn, can have their own secondary cords, and so on.

American historian Leslie Locke first decoded the knot system used in quipus in the early 1900's. These quipus record numbers using knots that indicate the values 0 through 9. The type and placement of a knot indicates whether it stands for ones, tens, hundreds, or some power of ten. For example, a group of four overhand knots in the tens position would indicate four tens, or 40. Any position empty of knots indicates a zero quantity of that power of ten.

A WRITING SYSTEM?

Most scholars believe that quipus record information only in the colors of the cord and the pattern of knots. Some researchers, however, have suggested that other features of the quipu may carry additional meaning. These include the manner in which the individual cords are woven and the direction in which the knots are tied. Some quipus do not always follow the numerical code described by Locke. A few scholars argue that these quipus use knots to record other information, such as historical accounts. They argue that the quipu represent a unique form of writing invented by the people of the Andes. However, scholars have not managed to fully decode any of these quipus.

Spanish conquistadors and priests destroyed many of the Inca quipus as they sought to wipe out the culture of the Inca. However, they did not manage to eliminate quipu from the culture of the Andes. As recently as the 1970's, Quechua-speaking shepherds of the Andes Mountains were still using the quipu to keep track of their flocks. Some Quechua communities in South America also preserve older quipus as part of their heritage. If they can be decoded, these quipus may provide clues about the traditions of local people prior to the Spanish conquest of the region in the 1500's.

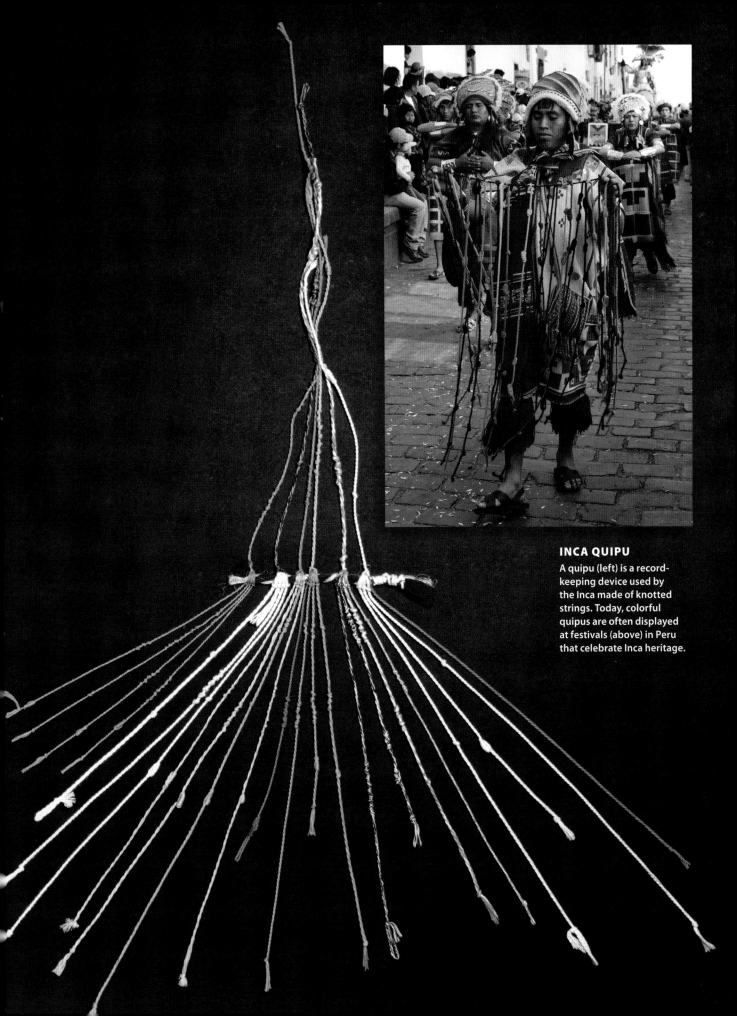

INCA QUIPU

A quipu (left) is a record-keeping device used by the Inca made of knotted strings. Today, colorful quipus are often displayed at festivals (above) in Peru that celebrate Inca heritage.

What Caused the Decline of Machu Picchu?

Machu Picchu was abandoned by the Inca some time after the Spanish conquered Cusco in November of 1533. The citadel may have been burned in 1550 during a Spanish expedition aimed at destroying Inca religious idols and ritual sites.

Historians believe that the few inhabitants remaining in Machu Picchu around 1540 fled quickly to avoid the risk of encountering the Spanish *conquistadors*. The invading Spanish had begun to penetrate the region around Vilcabamba, near the *sanctuary* (sacred place), where the remaining Inca who resisted Spanish rule had taken refuge.

However, Spanish histories from that time that may record the glory and the fall of this sacred place and its subsequent slide into oblivion are largely unknown. The Inca did not have written records as we understand them, and oral histories are rare and sometimes unreliable.

RELIGIOUS ZEAL
Peruvian historian Raúl Porras Barrenechea (1897-1960) has suggested that Machu Picchu may have been one of the first objectives in a campaign to wipe out the Inca religion, which Spanish priests viewed as pagan idolatry and devil worship. Spanish conquistadors did not hesitate to use fire in combat against the Inca and to utterly destroy any place sacred to them. Barrenechea wrote that "burning out the Incas" seemed to have been favored by the priests in the Vilcabamba area until about 1565. During his explorations in Peru from 1911 to 1915, Hiram Bingham was struck by the many indications that Inca sites were destroyed by fire, something that other *archaeologists* (scientists who study past cultures) also noticed in their investigations. Scholars think that after it was looted and burned by the Spanish, Machu Picchu was completely abandoned and eventually forgotten.

But other scholars suggest Machu Picchu was neither that lost nor that forgotten. Several Spanish documents mention locations that may, in fact, refer to the site. For example, in a document from 1562, "Pijchu" is mentioned as part of a land division entrusted to Hernando Pizarro. In May of 1565, Diego Rodríguez de Figueroa, who traveled in the Vilcabamba area and met with Inca rebels, spoke of "Picchu, which is in a peaceful area." The town of "Picho," listed in documents from 1568 found in the Archives of Cusco by Peruvian historians Luis Miguel Glave and María Isabel Remy, appears on a list of lands cultivated by the Inca in the Urubamba Valley. A notation that appears on this document indicates the town had been annexed and suggests it had been built by Pachacuti. Thus, it seems Machu Picchu was known, but the abandoned site was considered unimportant to the Spanish conquerors of Peru.

FORGOTTEN TEMPLE
The abandoned stone temple in a photo taken during Hiram Bingham's 1912 expedition.

FORGOTTEN TEMPLE
The abandoned stone temple in a photo taken during Hiram Bingham's 1912 expedition.

ABANDONED SITE
Vegetation grows from the sculpted stone in a place abandoned for centuries.

What Was the Treasure Found in Machu Picchu?

Much of the material taken from Machu Picchu by Bingham can be found at the Peabody Museum of Archaeology at Yale University. Though researchers usually speak of some 5,000 artifacts, the Peruvian government recently demanded the return of more than 46,000 pieces. The confusion stems from the fact that many objects are made up of many fragments. Only about 350 of these pieces are suitable for museum display. Yale University agreed to return these objects and an unspecified number of fragments as long as a suitable museum is built in Peru based on the standards given by Yale, so that the valuable objects will be properly preserved.

Places to See and Visit

OTHER PLACES OF INTEREST

CITY OF CUSCO
PERU

The ancient Inca capital is 74 miles (119 kilometers) from Machu Picchu and is the traditional point of departure for tourists visiting the ruins. In Cusco, you can visit the Museum of Pre-Columbian Art, the Coricancha Temple Museum (Temple of the Sun), and the current Plaza de Armas, once an Inca ceremonial site.

PÍSAC
PERU

This city is located 20 miles (32 kilometers) from Cusco, east of Vilcabamba. This is one of the end points of the Sacred Valley of the Inca, Ollantaytambo being the other. The city has a busy market and an astronomical observatory.

OLLANTAYTAMBO
PERU

Located 19 miles (30 kilometers) east of Machu Picchu, this city was the residence of Pachacuti, and it was later the center of the resistance led by Manco Inca Yupanqui. The train from Cusco to Machu Picchu travels through the city.

VILCABAMBA
PERU

Vilcabamba was the last refuge of the Inca. It was conquered in 1572, when the last emperor, Túpac Amaru, was executed. Located about 30 miles (48 kilometers) west of Machu Picchu, today the city is called *Espíritu Pampa* (Spirit of the Plain).

Machu Picchu

HOW TO GET THERE

The ruins can be visited any day of the year. Most visitors travel to Machu Picchu from the capital Lima, with a domestic flight to Cusco. From there, a train takes visitors to Aguas Calientes, also known as Machu Picchu Pueblo. From there, it's a short half-hour by bus to the site via Hiram Bingham Highway. The Manuel Chávez Ballón Museum is right next to Ruins Bridge and holds some 200 stone, metal, and ceramic objects from the Inca culture.

PROTECTED AREA

Machu Picchu was declared a UNESCO World Heritage Site for both its cultural and natural resources. The protected area contains an abundance of flora, including numerous species of orchids, and several unique species of animals, such as the giant hummingbird, the spectacled bear —the only bear in South America— and the Andean cock-of-the-rock, the national bird of Peru.

SEASON

As the most-visited tourist destination in Peru, receiving almost a half-million visitors per year, Machu Picchu can be crowded in the summer. Its location, at the top of the mountain and surrounded by the Urubamba River, means one should plan a trip carefully. Visiting during the rainy season, December to April, is not recommended. June and July are the coldest months there.

Inca Trail

People who wish to immerse themselves fully in the Andes and the world of the Inca can travel to Machu Picchu on foot, following part of the road built by the Inca themselves between Machu Picchu and an area outside of Cusco. The trail takes two to four days to walk. Along the Inca Trail are many archaeological sites, such as Llaqtapata, Huayllabamba, or Runkuraqay, in addition to an extraordinary landscape that ranges from the high mountains to the plains.

CHOQUEQUIRAO
PERU

Choquequirao is considered Machu Picchu's sister city, with a similar architecture and layout. Its name means "cradle of gold," and it is about 20 miles (32 kilometers) southwest of Machu Picchu. Although it cannot compete with Machu Picchu, it has the advantage of being less crowded. But, a two-day journey on foot is required to arrive at the site.

CHINCHERO
PERU

Chinchero is located 17 miles (27 kilometers) from Cusco and was at one time the royal palace of Topa Inca Yupanqui, Pachacuti's son and successor. The current inhabitants built their homes on top of the Inca ruins. The Sunday market and the church are the major tourist attractions.

PEABODY MUSEUM OF ARCHAEOLOGY
NEW HAVEN, CONNECTICUT

This Yale University museum houses and displays the Inca treasures taken from Peru by Hiram Bingham during his expeditions in 1912 and 1915. In 2010, Yale University agreed in principle to the return of the treasures to their original home in Peru. But the museum has yet to return the objects and continues to display them.

Glossary

Aclla— A term meaning *chosen woman* in the Quechua language.

Acllahuasi— A term meaning *house of the chosen women* in the Quechua language.

Amauta— Philosophers or wise men who advised the Inca ruler.

Apu panaca— The Inca officials responsible for selecting the acllas, or chosen women.

Aqueduct— An artificial channel or large pipe for bringing water from a distance.

Archaeology— The scientific study of the remains of past human cultures.

Artifact— Anything made by human skill or work, especially a tool or weapon.

Chicha— A fermented beverage made from corn, sugar cane, and other plants by Indians of South America.

Citadel— A high-walled fortress or city.

Computed tomography (CT)— An advanced type of X ray.

Conquistador— A Spanish conqueror in North or South America, especially during the 1500's.

Coya— The Inca emperor's main wife.

Divination— The act of foreseeing the future or foretelling the unknown through signs, objects, or events.

Dynasty— A series of rulers who belong to the same family.

Equinox— Either of the two times in the year when the sun crosses the equator, and day and night are of roughly equal length on all parts of the Earth.

Excavation— The act or process of digging up.

Hanan— An Inca term for the sacred district of a city, where temples and other religious sites were located.

Huaca— For the Inca, any object or place that possessed sacred or religious power.

Hurin— An Inca term for the residential portion of a city.

Illa—Small religious statues kept in Inca households.

Mallquis— Among the Inca, mummified family members kept and worshipped by their descendants.

Mamacona— An Inca priestess.

Mita— A tax in the form of labor that all Inca commoners contributed to the ruler.

Mummy— A body that has been carefully preserved through natural or artificial means.

Myth— A story of unknown origin, often one that attempts to account for events in nature or historical events from long ago.

Oracle— A wise person, one skilled in foretelling the future.

Quechua— The language and name of the main ethnic group of the Inca empire.

Quipu— A cord with knotted strings of different colors, used by the Inca to keep accounts.

Rural— Of or having to do with agriculture or farmland.

Sanctuary— A sacred place or refuge; the Inca kept their mummies there.

Solstice— Either of the two times in the year when the sun is at its greatest distance from Earth's equator.

Terrace— A flat, stepped platform of land, with a vertical or sloping front.

Tawantinsuyu— The Kingdom of the Sun, the Inca name for their empire.

Tribute— A required payment of goods or services made to the ruling authority by subjects.

Zancu— A bread of corn and blood used by the Inca as a religious offering.

For Further Information

Books

Hemming, John, and Edward Ranney. *Monuments of the Incas*. London: Thames & Hudson, 2010. Print.

Meinking, Mary. *Machu Picchu*. Minneapolis: Essential Library, 2015. Print.

Weil, Ann. *The World's Most Amazing Lost Cities*. Chicago: Raintree, 2012. Print.

West, Tracey. *Temple Run: Race through Time to Unlock Secrets of Ancient Worlds*. Washington, D.C.: National Geographic, 2014. Print.

Websites

"Ghosts of Machu Picchu." *Nova*. PBS, 2 Feb. 2010. Web. 25 Feb. 2015.

"Machu Picchu." *BBC Travel*. BBC, 2015. Web. 25 Feb. 2015.

"Machu Picchu." *History.com*. A&E Television Networks, 2015. Web. 23 Feb. 2015.

"Machu Picchu." *National Geographic*. National Geographic, 2015. Web. 25 Feb. 2015.

Index

Acknowledgments

Pictures:

© Alamy Images

AP Photo

© Corbis Images

© Cordon Press

© Getty Images

© iStockphoto

© Scala Archives